I0759572

Tantrums in Air

Emily Skillings

The Song Cave

for Lois, my mother,
and for Faye, her mother,
(whom I never met
but find I am meeting always
in my mind
or the world)

The Song Cave
www.the-song-cave.com

Author photo: Sarah Wagner Miller
Cover image: *A Quiet Pattern*, by Ebecho Muslimova
Design and layout by Janet Evans-Scanlon

ISBN: 979-8-9912988-0-3
Library of Congress Cataloguing-in-Publication Data has been applied for.

FIRST PRINTING

CONTENTS

You say that you do not know how to think. Yes; you do a little.

—Mary Wollstonecraft, “Lessons”

ROSE-CROWNED NIGHT GIRL

I am pointless. This I come to know
by pressing ear to night's machinery.
Outside, the words rub each other
until they are dull: calibrate, resurface,
surface, invest, investigate, snowy, open,
environ, woman, wooden, system.
I look where little nodes of language cling,
lichen-like, to what will have them.

The air framed beyond the high window
is an invitation. I could grab something.
Sample the pie and salad. I could recite
what I play at knowing, be disassembled
by an institution or human person,
could get inside a tree and take up position
as one who with her yellow eye stalks form.

I didn't know I was looking for it, but sure,
but sure. A chemic silver, a thought
darting through another's wet plumage.
Must I convene myself again?
And it is mournful, the recognition
of one's own phrase—a headless fish,
width of some finger, writhing,
cemented there.

PRELUDE: A LUMP OF PURE SOUND

As I set out to write—as I wrote—I asked myself, *am I stupid*? The thought appeared like a gold leap, it rushed from somewhere only to sit in tissue. It festered there. *Could I be stupid*? It wasn't new. The question had increased in potency and frequency. I had been taught by women not to pay attention to this thought. That the men had given it to me. My condition was caused by the men and the institutions they dominated that poisoned me into thinking I was an impostor. But I had always been an impostor. A fake. When I was a ballet dancer learning modern dance, I copied the looseness of dancers' limbs and sockets, the mannerisms of release. I watched videos of people with training to approximate my own, having learned none of the techniques of letting go. This was how I'd learned everything. By mimicking others until I could be, for a little while, unsupervised in movement and thought. To deny this would be a lie. I felt betrayed by the insistence that I was not a fraud. The shape and dimensions of the space that your body takes up as you move, as you walk and dance—measured from the most distal points of your limbs—is referred to as *kinesphere*, a term coined by Austrian movement theoretician Rudolf Laban, who invented a system of choreographic notation. He would later play a major role in the movement choir demonstrations of the Nazi Party. What is the kinesphere of my dull brain, my leaping body? I do not want one at all. I see a single oat, tumbling. When I was done with the dancers, I moved on to the poets. As a poet you never had to be anything, since whatever you did was pretty much fine. I wrote a few poems. Then a book. It was published. People read it. I began to teach, as one does. When I taught poetry I could get caught at any moment. I didn't know anything. I love literature but hadn't studied it in a serious way. A student points out a line in a contemporary poem cribbed from *Paradise Lost*. I have never bothered to read Milton. I once read the section where Eve wakes up, but I don't remember any of it. I read it because my friend told me it possessed "insane beauty," and that's not the kind of thing you ignore. In preparation for an interview to teach at a university, my former professor sat me down and told me how Milton called rhymed verse "the invention of a barbarous Age." I forgot to mention this at the interview, but I repeat this later to the students, without ever having read Milton's introduction. It wouldn't matter if I had. I read things and they float away. I would rather stare at my own breasts. "Mind like a steel sieve," my father would say. Yet I do know some things, I do understand. *I do not have to be smart*, repeated something within me, its insistence a kind of dull whimper, as from a child. *I am a poet.* "Poets are something else," Eileen Myles once wrote. I thought I'd found a haven where I could be half thinking, half nothing. I will not RSVP for a conference on anything at all. My students email me asking for things because I seem nice. They do not know I am bad. I say, "Yes of course." When it comes to their poems I want to say, "Just do whatever you want." At the faculty party, I walk away from the conversation about Mr. Heidegger, whom I do not understand, toward one about furniture, which I think about all day. I wish I could make a chair, but I don't have the energy to learn. Of course I am being defensive. Passive-aggressive, even. Why stop now? I think prose introduced the problem. I had to write about a dead man, a man I love who is dead. He was smarter than me and he was smarter than you. Writing prose was like crawling into my own grave and looking up at the sky. A brown tunnel with a scrap of blue at the end. Or it was like trying to catch snakes made of loose earth. Things seem close yet far away. The poets fucked me, wanted to fuck me for a while, they fell in and out of love with me. They sent me messages late at night and I rehearsed each reply like I was preparing for an examination. They texted screenshots of poems I was supposed to have known by now and I Googled the lines to see who they were written by. "I love this poem," I would reply, "one of my favorites." I see now how I thought being with them was part of what made me one of them, but I never said this out loud, because of course it is a stupid thought. On a date with a nice poet at some launch party for a literary journal I said a very famous poem by James Merrill was by some other poet. I think about this for months; in the dark, my face turns red and then drains. I do like Merrill's poem about the waterfall: *There is a chamber of black stone. High and dry behind my stunning life.* A different poet once told me I never talked about literature while we were together. I was teaching Kafka to freshmen and had paused, excitedly, on the section about the wound. Blooming with worms. They weren't there and then they were, poking in and out of the flesh of the little story. "But I talk about literature all the time," I said, staring into him like a basin full of rainwater. "Of course, of course you do." The water has filtered through all life, all horrible thought. The prose writer writes poems, essays, and novels, writes books I wish I knew how to write. She uses words I do not know. Has studied with French and German philosophers. At the party, the timid girl has taken too much cake (the icing an iridescent, living green; it spreads and spreads like tender shoots of clover) and cannot put it back, nor can she eat it all. There is dirt under my fingernails. I want to get very drunk in a dress and be loud. The tears lift off the pages of my homework, returning to my eyes. The symbols un-smear. "Good," says my father. "Now how do you solve for Y?" It is impossible. *Could I be stupid?* Perhaps one way forward was to consider the thought like an object. To give it my full and loving attention. To sit with it like a kind of pet or a child and see what it could teach me. I would invite it in for a year. We were inside a plague. The television and the radio spewing. Here is my furniture. Here is what I know. Sit. Don't run away. I felt highly oxygenated, high on the relief of the possibility. *Now you've seen through me, sang the cataract.* I, a kind of stunned worm, would sleep gluttonous in the stinking hole of the question. See, that was such a stupid thing to have written.

THE FOOL

I, too, long for a cradle
Of brilliant grasses
Braided through with wildflowers
Rocking on a historic mound
That drinks the blood of men
Clots of irreverent sight—
A shadow spills out
Of a pinprick
In the form

Down below on the hill
The men gasp and gurgle
Until they go out
Their weapons flirting in the sunshine
Slick with insides
The grasses grow strong and toxic
So goes my life
A kind of primitive cinema
A phantasmagoria
Shuddering toward the ultimate goal
Passed down through generations
Of whisperers, liars, mothers,
Scrapbookers, clowns
To extract the alien life-form that is desire
And drown it

Do you know who I am?
I have some names. You pick.
One of them is Alice
One of them is Trudy
My name is Bunny
I'm called Pearl, "The
Inheritor." Some call me
The Next One. My name is
Went to Market
Didn't you know?
Hello, hello
It's me, Virginia!
Actually it's Olive Oyl
Calliope's foolish little hyperlink
Slightly drunk on the thin stripes
Of neon fat astride
The tops of clouds

The sky is cold and unlikely
When I go on the airplane
I get all funny
Start thinking about vessels
Where I end and where light
Ends. What I contain
What contains me—*Miss*,

Can I please have some juice?
Nine swallows
Of triple-distilled vodka
Two pink packets of sweetener—

I'll flick them vigorously
Like a tiny bag of drugs—
And bring me Dryden's Virgil, a roasted lemon
Green ball of primordial fire
A cup of ice
Some nail glue

Arriving in the dead of air
Unstoppered, low on fumes
I know I can be hard to understand—
Not entirely reasonable—things
Can start to feel a little silly—forgotten—
I've forgotten what—exactly what—*Hey*!
    a strange figure
    nuzzles my outline
    I'm beginning to think
    that *long ago*
    I got stuck in a poem
    your poem
    and grew weary
    and lay down and slept
    and perished there
    it's not entirely unpleasant
    bursts, itches of flowers
    painting their lines
    dividing up my things
    I can feel them growing
    over me, covering me
    entering me
    even now

THE DUKE'S FOREST

> What more is there to do, except stay? And that we cannot do.
>
> —John Ashbery, "The Instruction Manual"

I love nature
but I think it awakens in me
intensely boring thoughts
that in the moment seem deep ravines
and when revisited later
have lost the light and dark greens
the wet wood and expansiveness.
See there I go sniffling.
I'm an American in Germany
at the edge of a public forest.
Today families were out walking.
The phrase "taking my constitutional"
something I've never said aloud
kept waving its little kerchief in me.
I walked four miles alone, feeling very pleased
with myself. *I wish a sweater*
could come in that shade of neon moss
I thought at one point, before entering a clearing
to gasp at a primal energy
that indoors now seems silly and evacuated.
In the Duke's Forest I find myself listing
names of plants it has omitted

the morning refreshingly flowerless
no lady slippers, oxlip, wood sorrel
no violets or ghost orchids.
I could go on. I go on.
This is why I love James Schuyler.
He doesn't care
that "the plants against the light
which shines in"
is a dull observation. Or that
"Trees, and trees, more trees"
is just the layered visual experience
we all have in the forest, waiting
to let ourselves take in the sign
to turn back, go home
and really hate someone.
Most days I stay as close to bed
as possible, even in my mind.
I trust my brain when she's indoors
and can bounce the materials
that seem to float toward and away
steadily, in equal measure
creating a kind of scrim
of thought over the body
off the surfaces of a room
mirrors, chairs, passages
from books, the objects
that ask me daily
to love them. They soak in
my attention and return it.
As color? Out in the woods

there is a refreshing smell
of decay. Today I saw
nine pussies in the trees.
One was forest art, carved
by someone I felt I'd already met
(it held a wooden jewel or egg
inside it, the size of a football
which I manipulated hesitantly
with my hand). The other eight
were "naturally occurring."
On my little walk I scratched
my asshole vigorously
right in front of a German family:
Mama, Papa, two kids, two
little white dogs. This gave me
great energy. I broke
off the path of the Hutewald
to access a large, termite-ridden tree
climbing into its opening
leaning back like you might do
on a long bus ride. The feeling is gone.
There was a weak and clotted stream just beyond
and beyond that a tree had fallen
no, broken in half (the trunk
still firmly rooted)
many years ago
and was carved to look like
the top of the base
and the bottom of the top half
are interlocking, a single

chain-link
connecting the two.
It's actually hard to describe
what this looks like
this cloven looming thing
the smart wicked from me
mind of wild dirt holes.
Perhaps you will see something better
wood embracing at the wound
of separation. In Paris I bought you
The Morning of the Poem
at that tourist trap bookstore
because you'd previously
expressed your skepticism
re: my devotion to it, as you tend
to question the value
of things I love. You became drunk
and silly on it
the opposite of my intended effect
began buying yourself cut flowers
and placing them in the window
to take their picture.
It seems you are now quoting extensively
from one of my favorite works
of American poetry
in a long poem you are writing
to another woman. My student just wrote
a brilliant and impossible poem
in which the forest extends to include
and contain everything, so that a forest

becomes indefinable, a catchall
container for experience, detritus,
life. He writes "And when I say forest,
I do not exclude," then seemingly lists
everything that has ever existed
in the physical world
beginning with spaces
like highways, medians, estuaries,
meadows, parking lots, drainage
ditches, clearings, and continuing on
toward sprawling lists of garbage,
thoughts, feelings, "piss-sprayed
shorts," the lost objects
of an entire national consciousness.
I'm so jealous of this poem.
But the thing about being outside
you can't really stay there.
It's getting a little late
and the panic light
is seeping in at the edges.
I'm in the dark of a library
with slightly bacterial wallpaper
reading men I love.
When I say that
I do not exclude you.
It had been so long.
Though it hurts (blasts) me
repeatedly, unendingly
I want to go back home.
A feeling with many thresholds

with many names.
So that when he writes
"Night slams gently down"
I am not my own way.
I am far from my own ways.

AN ENVIRONMENTAL POEM

I think to send pictures
of the brick-colored ones
spotted and
with stalks fatter than their little heads
to the amateur mycologist
with the questionable beard.
He told me to read a book
called *The Extended Mind*
and how a bird's nest
is considered by certain experts
to be an extension of its brain and being.
Or was it its DNA? I can't be entirely sure
as the great lawn stretches before me
waving me out
until it is interrupted by the road
full of the ghostly trails
of parcels and people
and what carries them
each journey an underline that reinforces
like a fattening braid of habitual fibers
its being there. How awful
there is a road before me.
How awful there is a house behind me.
Its bottles and food,
dulling syrups, devices, its chemicals,
the imprisoned plants and shapes

of yielding plushness, paintings
of the sea. Must one climb back into its clutches?
The duvet white and cloying as foam.
The other option is to go "somewhere."
But that is where that lizard bitch lives
with her rich stepbrothers, the floods,
to carry her. I wear a silk garment
studded with miniature islands
receding into a turquoise ocean.
Inside, the climate control leaps into action.
A tracking number moans into my palm.
Today I have tried to make a poem a trap
of twigs and mud, where I am encased
and decay. I press against the walls
until they are curved by my curving breast
which pricks against the sharpness
of what I've collected
producing little pains, open words,
constellations that touch no myths,
futureless calligraphies.
Until my robe is shredded.
Until the blood weeps down.

TENANT

Thomisidae

Crablike
it uncloaks
from itself—
removes
its own ghost-
ly paper. A leg
of mostly air
remains in air.
The hollowed
onionskin bulbs
where eyes once lay
look out on the field.
The din of it.
A new body
is painful. Exposed,
it must retreat
what was once inside
further inside.
Globe perched
on translucent needles,
the articulated twin
chooses tomb or home.
It violates a form.
Bud like a fist.

Like a thought
about to give
out. There is a pink
so clear and pale
a rose can't
call it kin.
A dwelling clutches
close to itself—
its what?
Its brief solitude
before welcoming
the traveler
to crawl
the repeating galleries
to wait in holy center.
It drags
the outside there.

READING

She'd always, The Student, underlined in her books, dog-
eared the pages. It was as if without these markings
she couldn't understand what was written, couldn't feel
the words alive in her mind. The blueblack liquid
corralled, as it dried, the text into something concentrated,
something a bit her own. A garden
drying in the sun, wrung out, pressed by the sky
's knowing. This was as much a part of reading as seeing.
She brought to each book her small void,
bouquet of nothing, a vase-shaped, cut glass lack
and would stuff it up with passages, themselves tunnels
elsewhere. The rest of the book, it seemed, could disappear,

and she would still possess some part of it. Was this
another book altogether, she thought, her book? At night,
on special occasions she could not induce at will, the words
would turn color—a red insulated by a thin border of spring
green—and hover slightly off the page, as if the paper
had released its hold, was handing the words over to her. They seemed,
these letters, to tremble—Christmas gelatin. She'd shake
her head to exaggerate this phenomenon, a private dance,
a direct communication from the writer, or, even better,
from the secret soul inside the book (that all books possessed).
More probable, she knew, something was wrong
with her eyes. They were reading *The Scarlet Letter*

and Ms. Russell, her 10th-grade teacher, pulled her aside after a failed quiz.
When something important happens on the page, she said,
choose a word or phrase that corresponds and write it
at the top, so you remember. The Student began with Chapter 10: "Torture"
she wrote in the blank and yellowing space on page 117, "appearances
and reality" (129) "she has removed the sin from herself"
"rebellion returning" (160) "limbo again" (174) "Pearl wants
the letter back" (192) "What did he whisper" (201) and then, simply,
"Seeing" (206). This went on forever. Well into adulthood, she wondered
if these words were the right ones. Sometimes a hole would appear,
moving its blurry center wherever she hauled her eyes. Words slipped
over the edge, withdrawing to a forest where she could not follow.

ELECTRIC

In the dream I wrote this poem called "Electric."
Somehow I got the *t* in the middle of the title
to wiggle. All the words of the poem
were crossed out with clay-colored lines
that ran through like fences or wires.
I could only see the tops and bottoms of the letters.
When I scraped the words of the poem with a knife
like a scratch card, the text remained hidden
behind opalescent scars
which hovered and shifted "cloudlike"
wherever my eyes rested. I put the shavings
under a big lens, and it seemed to me that was the real poem.
I remain unsure of what it said. The sound attached was red,
almost "a berry caught in an engine." I do not think
I want to write anymore. I haven't in many months.
One line occurs to me and repeats. It will not make way.
But here, still, is the knife in my right hand.

SCREEN TEST

I couldn't see great so I cut open the air in front of my face. Inside the little slit was a dense forest, partially occluded by gaps of fog. I hated my life. I was 31. "Can I record you?" asked a voice from inside the lushness of the foliage, "I'm making a documentary for my class on the subject of giant losers." The hole blinked. "Record me doing what?" I asked, already tired, the image of a desert flashing on some internal screen that in such moments shows me—and whoever else is watching—what I will never possess. "It doesn't matter," said the gap, "you could do, say, anything and you would still be yourself. It's that pathetic essence I've just got to capture for my work."

In the desert, a group of people were sitting on plastic furniture around a large, roasting carcass. A man got up to fill a cup of liquid from a cooler, walked it over to a woman, rubbing the top part of her back, his hand lingering in the creamy fibers of her sweater. A muted electronic pulse—gentle music—ascended to create a dome of contentment over the scene. My fantasies were outgrowing me, as if painted by someone in the future, kept in a dark hall of landscapes: deserts, forests, meadows, coves, ruins, all suspended in gesture, each color reaching toward me through its own substance of attention.

"Hey! I don't have all day," whined the hole. A fern shook off a few loose droplets, which were eagerly absorbed by a carpet of reddish topsoil. "Give me your answer. I really need this to work out for me, and I think I've hit the jackpot with you."

Thoughts of the bad thing were beginning to stir in me, the thing that happened that time and could happen again without warning. The woman looked up from the fire and the poor animal scenting the air, whose drippings of liquid fat sent small explosions into the night. It had been unfair for Frank to bring her here, knowing what he did. "Which cliff will we visit tomorrow," she asked no one.

I thought of rain. No sound. The happy worms drinking, rehydrating in the earth.

"Sure," I said. "Go ahead," I said, stroking the sore little burn waiting patiently in my mouth.

BALUSTRADE

a ballet in four acts

I. Toccata

If the group is modern, where are they going?
Cutting across the field, up that coquettish hill,
toward what, a city, a stone school built by workers
where things go to be disassembled? Lines jut out
from what we label. Little troupe of joyous exactos,

sexual in the checkered light of afternoon,
beaming into the words we grasp at
but ultimately forget. An activated zone
where things go to be disassembled. Lines jut out
from the urn, the string of glass beads, the stopwatch,

an encyclopedia of ranked pills. I found the night to be hot,
uncomfortably so, and so did what we all do, folded back
a corner of the sheet so my feet could be "free as Frenchmen,"
a stupid phrase I've never understood. The flower water had clouded,
a pond of milk on the corner table into which the moon died

incrementally. I was there, where I last looked. Now I'm here.
I'm not alone. What merges us to the journey, the movie—a liquid costume
emerges and we stand while it encapsulates us "slowly but Shirley,"

a stupid phrase I've never understood. The flowing water was cultlike,
demanded obedience. I attempted to rejoin the moving plot

that had continued on in my absence.
The group was on a hike, a tour of the history of montage,
braiding themselves through the woods, each phrase a casting off
(a gesture as much about seeking as it is about letting go)
between the trees, on which were projected thousands of scenes

made up of smaller scenes. It felt organic, casual, yet impossibly constructed.
Did the trees secrete these images? I saw no equipment. "Stop it,"
said the soloist. "You're overthinking." She placed her hand between
    my breasts
(a gesture as much about seeking as it is about letting go)
and I realized I had been one among women for some time.

"This will change soon," she said. A clearing dilated before us,
a platter of painted grasses. I had learned of such spaces
in books I'd neglected to read. They were essential to selfhood
and being with others—something to do with true emptiness and sight,
and how both were necessary in order to fully emerge, as the opening chord

pierces through silence. But was this space made by us,
or did it just *happen*? "Look" said a cousin, pointing to the center
at a quarry hidden by tall flowers. Reflected in the water was a saying
    we all knew,
something about being with others, emptiness, and sight. I looked up
from the italicized language to my surrounds. My friends
were a semicircle of statues, frozen in the clearing,
kneeling at slightly different levels. Marble, exeunt. Let go of my wet eyes.

II. Aria

the countless spines
of trees flare up

against a dark backdrop
the man and woman bow

to the sacred altar
of the other's bow

the movement is more of an admission
they are living in the same time

you are my contemporary
and in attitudes

we have been similarly trained
towards evasion and chance

"I don't care," I say vigorously
"Nor do I!" you say

with an intensity of feeling
akin to crowning oneself

in the briefest garden
a tantrum of flowers at our feet

and it's easy to explain
you want to take my hand

but it has become
property of the museum

though I work against it
a thought moves in:

so much is presumed, filled in
by gossip among the senses

I fear I will always be tired
and dumb, that I will never be released

from the repetitions of men
my mother told me to change

my earrings every day. "Change
your earrings every day," she told me

it seemed to me this was a sort of project
or assignment re: variation and choice

the ornament "pierces"
where there is already a lack, so the act

is more of a historical reference
to a past violence

than a violence itself—
a commemorative ceremony

performed daily to the sound
of smashed enclosures opening

to greet the air
where once I was wounded

now there is nothing but entry
the leg penetrates the circle the arms make

one day you asked me to haunt
the back of my own knee, to picture

the muscles of my legs and groin
as plastic drinking straws

through which lightness could be drawn
up into a crown

to set the voyage of my gaze
just beyond my middle finger

instead of at the wall
its novel of peeling paint

one day you asked me to "go on"
to continue, to "do it again," to push

deep into the vertiginous exactitudes
always slightly out of reach

when I found I could not
I gathered quietly my things

and left without ceremony
I became a different kind of person

part ghost, part sponge
a lump of pure refusal—

who extinguished the hot white frill
that wicked life into life?

often the wrists are grasped
so the pair may counterbalance

often the courtly and ancient light
is ground into the ground

III. Aria

The truth is that it's all terrible, and equally so, it's just the matter of
    choosing
which terrible to settle down with. This is the task from which we glance,

and to be frank, I would rather be in agony than even slightly bored.
    No. Reverse

that. The cartoon rat sits high on the lamp post, drinking a Miller High Life,

whistling "Jolene" into the alley below. *Weaving in and out of purple-black anguish*
and interstices of lightheartedness, the couple stabs the air with certain intensity.

"I'm begging of you, please don't take my man." *Do they move in a cipher?*
A kind of asemic pantomime of interdependence? Precariousness? If I admit I need you

in order that I may stand, may move, may hold my limb so exquisitely extending
like an echo emptying slowly its molecules into the middle distance, am I

the squeaking weakling? On our walk to the quarry at the edge of the world,
we saw trees choked out by vines. "Knotweed," you said. An "invasive species,"

you said. It poured out of the forest like many bitter fountains. I've seen the calm,
limp drape of a limb harden into insistence. *He rotates her delicately on her axis.*

She is at a slight angle. The first image that comes to mind is of a dead animal
being roasted on a spit. More accurate might be the act of turning an egg or rock

so that it is evenly warmed by the sun. To gently tilt and turn your lover toward the source of their suffering or their sustenance. Before you I am both meat and material,

a perfumed lozenge rolled around in the mouth to beat back the void sickness
until I disappear completely. *They are clipping along at a trot as if the sound of the forest*

isn't looming behind them, as if the stage isn't littered with dangerous holes. Rocks tumble
into the quarry's center pit. We say "at arms-length" to mean "held at a distance,"

but the length of an arm isn't really that far. Anything can be a distance. Even flesh-to-flesh
can seem a canyon's thickening waist. I suppose the dimensions of an embrace

become a measuring device. *Her arm attempts an ultimate boundary it fails again and again*
to enforce. I fight against the likely true assumption that we inhale like a breakfast:

that I am an impression and you are an idea. I would like to dress up as the idea for once,
its stately slacks and feathered hat, for I too was "born midsummer, already dying," a fact

I won't relinquish to this evening presenting itself like a fan before us, not without a fight.

She moves herself within his gate. I'm not sure I would like to be a feeling platform either,

nor to take up residence within the intimate contraption. When I say I need you to admit your
helplessness in order to stand across from you, you palm the knots in my cherrywood knees.

When you bend yourself back into unconsciousness you take me down with you. I open myself
to you, to the liquid field. I close myself again. *Their movement is like a sad door.*

IV. Capriccio

The great hall has stood for hundreds or thousands of years. If we agree
with what we have been taught by art, that "all space is contained inside us,"
that we are not Mary Poppins but, in fact, her magical bag,
then is there nowhere for us to go? It is for this reason

that we must enter as a group through the large, arched doorway,
that we must spear the breeze in faceted formation. Inside,
the intoxication of moving in unison combines with the sweet,
pointillist gestures of greeting someone you know as you approach them

from across the room . . .
When I first met my friends,
I was delighted to be embraced by poets and artists.
We were all in love with each other and for the first time in my life,

I felt I really belonged somewhere. We ate a lot of cheese and olives,
crackers embedded with fruit and hazelnuts, and downed ice-cold
gulps of white wine from tiny, elegant cups. We watched videos
and sang to each other, petting each other's hair while sitting on

handcrafted stools and textiles painted with ancient pictograms.
I was the youngest, a Pollyanna by nature, and the newest to the group,
and took up my place as a silly novelty (the role in which I have always felt
most comfortable). Everyone was a genius in their own way

and inspired the genius of the others. I took no lovers, as none were needed.
It was beginning to feel like something very exciting was about to happen.
Pink horses gathered against the orange horizon. The choir inhaled in
unison.
You know how the story goes. Someone crushed a chrysanthemum into
milk.

A succession of minor betrayals. Z saw a horned beast in K's coffee crystals.
The social braid we had created unraveled. I was forced to meet
my friends individually, which was not nearly as fun or intoxicating.
Crestfallen, I wandered around the windswept city like a child of divorce,

taking pictures with my phone and buying food. My reversible arms
still waved—my flippant limbs yearned for their corps. And there,
tucked into the tender folds of the avenues and their shops, I found
I was alone . . .

A dance instructor once asked me to picture a circle,
a hoop the size of a large wrist, that was half-embedded in my body

and existed half outside, the locus being my navel, like a planetary ring
or the gimbal of a gyroscope. Standing, I was to imagine using the circle

to draw in energy toward my "center" (from the air? my surroundings?)
and then release that same energy out into the world as I invited more inside.
When I moved I could increase and decrease the size of the circle as needed.
It could become as large as the room itself or as small as the pit of an apricot.

I liked the image but found the act to be pointless, as I was already breathing,
a quite similar yet functional necessity. A devotee of the "strange idea"
as a chance, fleeting encounter as opposed to a practice that is worked through
and integrated over time, I hesitated to assimilate the kinespherical gadget.

I now feel I made a huge mistake, but the attending sensation,
like a dilating engine, a pump exchanging the interior with the exterior,
cannot be retrieved. But isn't this . . . living? As always, possessing something
necessarily solves the problem of being without it, or so said Gilda

in the advertisement for the mysterious pink box on which the black triangle
was painted. "Thanks, Vicky. I never knew it was possible to be this sure of myself."
"Does it have a name?" "I don't know! It's just . . . I've never felt so impenetrable
or simultaneous in my whole life." A soft blow jostles

the flesh at play. Back in the hall
the dancers are marking a movement much like the clearing away or
harvesting
of cobwebs. Garlands are strung up between the pillars. Piles of
glistening food
topped with small green sketches and the petals of edible flowers are served

on platters resembling the reflective surfaces of mythic gazing-pools.
Mellifluous crossings streak the floor, as deer and bison etch their desires
onto fields.
To be casual and yet precise is the near-unattainable goal into which we dig
our collective heels. All moments incline their heads toward us now

with the expectation of a bloom. Sounds. Appetites. Tattered folders
bursting with snapshots. A system of tonal or polar centers. Postures
of complete readiness. But the content is nowhere to be found, or when found,
is "harsh in its newness." We like it this way, a comblike network of fences

embroidered into silk. And what of this motif bubbling underneath us?
The vaguely municipal odor of dust, wood polish, and decisions to be made
encircles the first menacing note of Spring. Fiddleheads unfurl through
the dirt.
And these tiles underfoot, they are beginning to show their cracks proudly,

like badges. If the sign could only make itself known, we could pack up,
return home on the path through the hills. Until then, I'm afraid, even
as the coolness
of evening tempts us to expire, we must keep ourselves moving. There
is nothing
in this expression that should frighten you. One must admit that all this

is not exactly clear. You pay perhaps too much attention to the notes in
my mouth.
The trees and daughters sound brightly tonight in the offices of difficult
music.

TANTRUMS IN AIR

blue blue reins
of the sun

lashed out
in licks

hot and cold as
voice poured through wire

a word flails
then loses grip

what would it take
to reach you
in this still air

in which I ride
on my black
wood horse

I could die here
in my poem

just to give it
a try. boom.

"guilt-free"
as they say

is it perennial or
perineum—and was she

astonished? Lady Time
with her nautilus head
cradling a glass

raspberry. Anesthesia
such a pretty name
for a girl

sometimes you flop over
like a fat carp inside me

or circle
as a finger

over a laminated menu
the broccoli rabe with chili

and lemon. I pre-mourn
my selfish time, my water hours

I take a small dictation
from you—sucking in and out
"lots of beautiful fluid"

the ultrasound tech
says to the beeping space
around my body

went to see her play
the long string instrument

somehow wasn't as long
as I'd hoped. She walked

on a track between wires
pinching delicately

the lines between
her fingers. She changed direction

so the sound would never end
I found myself watching
her feet most of all, their tentative

crossing. Most lines everywhere
too short.
I didn't write it. It was already there.

They were widowed images
Color pulled from sleep

The cloud like a vampire imp
Sucking his long fingers

Yes I want to protect my experience
(Recommended)

Is that where the light went
Attention shoved

Into a small box. Violences
Crept out, slowly at first
Then flooded each sinus

Nothing conceivable. The gray faces
of the dead. The land. No I don't want
My experience protected

burst of ill humor
our lady

has had some of her tanterums
as Vapors comeing out etc.

two hands, one
then the other, fall

onto stretched skin of drum
Be gone. Be gone.

Hate it here, says Zach. Want
to go home. A tall spike of grass
makes a scream, green shot high

into air. In storm's stirring, a tremor
in my runt eye—tears ripped out
like tansy flowers

Took so long
to write a book

It's embarrassing
the middle—how it stretches

on, how it smells, desperate
"Are your fingers

in the margin?"
writes Lyn Hejinian

in the middle
of a passage
in *My Life,* and

the first time
I read that I gasped
because, of course, they were.

the silver nipple hair
the nut-brown maid

the blown
the wooden turnip

the ring of muscle
the arc of fluid

the agate cave
the chisel unlocks

the huckleberry app
the data collected by each of
the tracking pixels

the undone morning
the unswept floor
the never, the not even once

Lie down gently your weary stalks.
Is it lay or is it lie? Remind me.

I lie myself at the feet of my savior.
Lay here on the cold slab of—

I lied, I never lay with him, but he did
Touch me upright, laying his fingers

On my clammy cheek. Lay eyes to the page
The words lie here. The words lay

Down in—are these the green pastures
Everyone's been talking about?
Now I lay me. Lie lady lie, lie across my weeping

lineage. I lay here afraid of what will come, pink sky
laying her droplets. Just lying around. You'll never learn
that way. Lay down. Down on your white belly.

turned
a
corner
to
hear
the
labored
ecstatic
song
of
the
twenty-
foot
drill

words stuck
like milk

clump of berry
calls to wind

ground me
my eye advances

then rears back
from the red shapes

the whitish sky
cannot possibly desire what
it already possesses

in its arms—make me
again angular, sometimes rosy,
once a stain

Ali turns to me. "Emily, sometimes I think I was hungry in the womb."

The carrot flower, or Queen Anne's lace,
is everywhere this summer.
I love it when they are as large
and white as a china saucer.
The period in the middle.
A little centering gesture.
A sip of dark, a hole
into which slips all
the sky's embroidery. The field,
the side of the road, the shrill path,
all show me the commonness of my form.
Before the pedicels flatten, they make a fist
Around whatever's coming. Today:
a broken nail, a sink drain, a warning.

How could I know
What I desire

I desire myself, or
Possibly a pink curtain

I can pull back
Behind it

Is a small bouquet
Inside the blooms

Their alien musk
Sits a microphone
Clipped to the lapel

Of a small god
They ask me a question
They take it all down

LADIES! BE YOUR OWN GRAVE

> "Rose red, in many variations of shade, dark in the hollows, lighter at the edges, softly granulated, with irregular clots of blood, open as a surface mine to the daylight . . . Poor boy, you were past helping. I had discovered your great wound; this blossom in your side was destroying you."
>
> —Franz Kafka, "A Country Doctor"

Ever since I was a little girl
I've always wanted to yell, "My leg!
My leg!" after a great accident.
In this fantasy I am myself
but also an old man in a golfing costume
walking alone down a country road
distracted by the slightly annoying and toxic
first green of spring, eyes overflowing
with the high-pitched, adolescent hum
that oft accompanies my idleness
when a large branch topples down on me.
Before this happens I am thinking of you
so in a sense you are the true accident.
"Crushed again!" I moan to no one
down in the dirt
where I have always belonged.
The ditch, she comforts me
her pocked surface a trove for sight

den mother for lichens, moss,
recesses in which frightened beetles
may withdraw from the day.
In our shared madness
the ditch and I
we stare together
deep into my wound.
I will describe it for you:
French Bible painted white
in which a slit is laser cut
down through the pages, almost to Job.
Smoked salmon inlaid with gravel-
bits on repurposed board.
Neoclassical detail
of a crumpled garment
left after a feast.
Maquette for a later work
done hastily in wine-colored Plastilina.
The red lace border acts
as a kind of shore.
The tilting mechanism
underneath the irregular bowl
reveals and conceals
a partially hidden core
of fossilized mammoth ivory.
Drawer overflowing with wet scarves.
Giclée print of stabbed Victorian
overstuffed chair. Raspberry sorbet
replaces the body
of the oyster.

Flipping through wallpaper swatches
you find your sister's mouth
breathing up at you. She spits
up the retainer you lost
on a school trip in 8th grade
down a museum's elevator shaft.
A screensaver in a dark room.
A mirror that reflects the room
without you in it. A chewing gum
vase. A song about falling
plays as you fall. The deep,
perfumed hole
lined with feathered rags
that has been forming
in the middle of 3rd Avenue
for some time now.
A hot little flower.
The faces of my bored students
during a screening
of Chantal Akerman's
La Chambre produce
a hurt in me not unlike this one.
Will you cup it in your mind?
Give her a little blow?
You'll be happy to know
that in this piece we are confronted
with the artist's struggle
to work inside limiting
yet often exhilarating
boundaries of femininity

as they relate to time,
duration, and landscapes
of the domestic interior.
And that's really something.
I guess the thing is
I would like an apology
for the last time we lay together
the way you touched me in a hurry.
I am looking out the window
at a handsome roofer
climbing a ladder. This rubber baby
purchased online from Idaho
arrived in tissue.
She cries real tears.

FANTASY

In this one
I am a snail
I am myself
But a snail
I circle the circle
Of a compact mirror, open
As a plastic clam
To the sky, my trail
Of slime
It blurs the mirror
So that the sky
Is smeared
Is wrecked
So that you could not see
Your own face
Even if you tried
To peer into
The cool surface
Feels so good
Against the me
I drag along
I sing
A pearly song
Erasing the clouds
Erasing your face
I know you want to feel me

Gliding
Wet over your cheek
But as you know, I am married
To the mirror, the circle
My brown spiral shell
The inscrutable sky

MAW

Like an erotic dream
in which I
in dark overalls
run over my body
a lint roller
until the argument
no sorry sorry
the garment
disappears completely
—sheets after sheets
of tacky black
jeté into the
mouth of the garbage—
I want to remove
the sun of you
from my stone
Emily said
they told her
she "wrote like a man"
was it in a class
or on paper
I think she was bragging
precisely because
I got so jealous
it was like a light
jacket thrown over
her shoulders

in 65 degrees
her foot casually holding open the door
after a question posed
to the person inside
not caring if they answer
the foot is removed
prematurely
oh bring me that rock
to smash me in I
would take any pill
to drown in green
to make nothing
the baby
the lover
the voicemail, the wasp
the electronic trace
at the curve of thought
that interrupts this
this hyperactive
wet vellum brain
get out, out
of here
get off
it feels so good
going through
I can't stop
you're dead now
or slightly eternal
the air of the answer
drinking it down

HEAVEN

> "Take the things you say because you can't write poems and figure out how to write some."
>
> —Dorothea Lasky, "The Poetry That Is Going to Matter After You Are Dead"

The line is all I have
Is my response
To you, one of these poets
Whose hatred of their art
Rests so thickly in the mouth
As to almost clog it
You who use poetry
As a kind of signal
But don't write it, not really
And think we should all
Be writing pert little essays
Or etching swollen fields of hyperlinks
Or archiving a leak from 1976
Don't you know you could be speaking
Directly to the dead
Like this, like I can
I am doing it now
I can tell
When you take a shit
Your feet up
On some low bamboo stool

So waste can better fall
From out your hole
You are weeping
Secretly into the spine
Of *The Age of Anxiety*
No, worse
Into the poet's fleshy back
The words grow wet
And begin to stink
Listen you skein of mold
You asbestos clown
You excuse you joyless
Sorrowless person
The line break is all
I have in this world
It is the mother
The wave and the undertow
The reconstituting cliff
I will jump from
My whole life
No matter how much
I want to end
I end up
Right back at the top
Staring out, face slightly perplexed
By the machine that returns my gaze
Her eyelashes heavy
With bees, or often
Snow. I know inside
The pour of this exchange

I will never die
I will just reappear
I will "GO OUT" in order
That I may "COME
TO," slipping under
The anesthesiologist's mirror
To swim the silver channel
Beyond recognition
That waits for me
Just on the other side
I'll get shot out, gasping
Into a cracked grotto
In which blue waters dance
Over the stones and moss
My hair all in clumps
Will soon dry
I am not even close
To beautiful, am dumb,
Or numb at least
I've no husband
Nor a career. No children
Pull at my flesh
Though heavily I am leaned
Upon. The break
The relentless coming of days
The do it again
And do it now, this
Is my heaven
I leave it
In order that I may return

Wearing this very crown
Of asemic darts
Why dance with invention
Everything is here already
The snake you know
Escapes his former skin
So that you might pick it up
And drape it in the direction
Of your voice. Listen,
Can you hear that whoosh
That is language turning over
It makes a sweet sound
Kicks up a scent from the dirt
It too is yours
You do not need any permission
Certainly not mine
But you, poet
You know this already
And in this moment, balancing
On the outer rim
You will give it up
For no one

DAPHNE

This thing happens
You write half a poem
And then stop
At the first sign of difficulty
So you have all these half-poems
The drooping heads of flowers
You call lilies as a placeholder
Stemless, waiting
Open-mouthed. To go back in
And look on them
Is something horrible
Better to forget they are there
Like the dream in which you know you've left
Your little baby all alone
If only you could recall where
And you're trying to stay positive
Was it under the pile of coats
Or in the closet
It needs the blue and meditative light
That runs from your body. Its name
The name of a flower, Dahlia,
Delilah? Oh the pitiful thing
Must be somewhere, shriveling
In a box, an atrophied pile of sound
There is a window
Opens onto a field

Opens onto a dancefloor, opens
Onto a graveyard
Rachel, your most glamorous friend
Muses that the present has become
For all children, an ambient gel
In which the catastrophic and the banal
Ride at indistinguishable frequencies
She passes you a glass
And soon Delia
Is only a nagging thought
You have worn the black blouse
Encrusted in sequins
The pattern, venereal
Pink, gold, blue,
They flash as you twist your bones
Inside their fleshy
And mostly biodegradable case
You repeat a movement
That is like wilting
At an accelerated speed
To remind onlookers
How you once wrote poems
In one there was a blender
Full of white glue
With a fly swimming in it
With a fly drowning in it
You could stick your hand in
Press "pulverize" or "pulse"
But to what end
You've neglected the paperwork

All your life
Beyond the door, the grass is wet
The lawn strewn with what
You can’t entirely say

GARGOUILLADE

If, as I suspect, all language has died
for me, at least for the time being, then I'll trot
out the little reeking phonemes,
the dancing spines, the disremembered—
and I promise I will not try. Someone smells amazing
at the weird art party
where I am asked to read poetry
to looping electronic music.
I want to be a poet entirely
of a different kind. Later I discover
the scent is coming from the scrawny potted jasmine
blooming in the corner, dropping her
syrup on the floor. It's nice to meet a fellow
whore in the world.

A POTENTIALLY GOOD BOOK SOAKED IN OFFENSIVE PERFUME

The poet may well be wonderful, as her website and excerpt in *Harper's* suggest. However, it's not to be discovered because the distributor, for whatever misguided reason, has saturated the book in a chemical citrus scent that wafts chokingly off each turned page and brought on an allergy attack in my case. The arrogance with which business people contaminate art with the marketing ploys of their approach is epitomized here—and however delicate the scent to those not offended, its production backstory invokes landscapes of smokestacks, tanker trucks, chemical vats, game animals butchered for their glands, and endless laboratory corridors of torture-tested domestic pets bent and broken to the service of people who'd olfactorily intrude on the sensora of others with the myriad corporate odors with which they cover up their imagined animality and style their constructed personalities, not often so offensively as when the pursuit of literature is thus contaminated. Does the poet know? Or was it maybe her idea? Too bad.

TRAIPSE

The impossible word
sloshes around,
a mood looking for an exit
and seaweed gets on the clock, a bit
of silt at six's curve.

There is no finish on the day
it just kind of slumps over
and there's another one
to stab you like a cartoon predator
with a blade of straw
which just a moment ago
waved, long and golden
from the mud slit
between teeth.

I feel I'm supposed to be monitoring something.
But what exactly?
I see your outline, your shadow jaw
better in the dark
as the hermit crab crawls
between LCD screens.
What choice have I?

I could die from sadness—
green, powdery, and collecting

in the low places where everyone hates me.
I've been so bad, so wrong.

He gets me with a mallet
at the base of a tree.
The black cloud of smoke that emerges
is my childlike wonder leaving
to perfume
our postcard backdrop. Hello
from wherever
the hell this is.
I'm calm.

VOICEMAIL FROM THE IMPALED

after Ebecho Muslimova

The branch goes into my vagina
and exits my mouth.
Like sellers of fine carpets, leaves unfold
their new colors at my lips.
The lovers walk the scrawny path
to visit at their assigned hours.
The one who is meanest is the one I most love.
He brings me a fish full of needles.
I am happy to provide
for everyone whatever they need,
as everything outside
swirls thickly and dark.
My holes rotate positions.
A strong stain is created
by the fears of others.
It tints the sky; her lilac iris watches.

I'm stuck here, here
Where I have asked you to come.
You are no friend.
My only one is the dog there.
The good blood dripping
from his mouth, fast like a trill,
is a novel full of ideas.

The wind's iron fingernails
brush back sweetly my hair
from my face. It's true,
we gave something up
that was not ours to give.
Is my ear the shape of a question?
The scene exchanges my blood
for a sound. Even the worms
grow drunk on it.

GLOBES

That terrible autumn
when I bled
I turned toward beauty
like one turns their cheek
into the advancing plane
of a slap. The number
and small address
for a hematologist
or two, brother docs
at the same clinic,
sprawled beneath the notes
for a poem, a kind of symbolic grove—
the harvest of red and brown globes
glowing quietly
impenetrable under frost.
My mouth was white inside
the chilled landscape.
I had been trying to think
like a dead man, but was neither,
so for so long went unthinking.
A single red fox
slinked its hungry form
along the curve
of my eyelid. It is now,
I thought, that you must attend
to the story of your unfortunate body.

Hello Dr. Allen, hello Dr. Dave,
will this vine
that connects all with all
or most with most, or some
with some
but not others
shatter
when first I stoop to touch
its frightening green?

IDEA FOR THE BEGINNING OF A NOVEL

The pills had been delivered,
though she'd not been home
to receive them. They were sitting there
in a white paper bag, stapled shut
with her name on it: a popular given
followed by a strange and slightly severe word
and the date of her birth,
a humid day in August of 1988,
printed next to the instructions
which might, she thought,
mention milk
or heavy machinery.
She pictured the parcel on the small table,
with its rounded corners
and the chairs that fit cleanly over them.
"My boyfriend's upstairs.
You can ring the bell,"
she'd said to Rick, a man
a company called Rx2Go
had sent to deliver medicine
all over Brooklyn, "and he'll come down
to fetch them." Rick's voice was sweet but professional,
and as he'd asked for the apartment number,
her train, scraping through Connecticut,
passed a small inlet
crowded with twenty or so egrets

posed differently, otherwise identical,
like a gallery of sculptures of the same god
made of the same shimmering white stone.
"I live in apartment 3,"
she'd answered, "but there is no need to climb
the stairs. He will come down."
It was starting to rain.
Her neighboring commuter
abandoned her book
for games of disappearing, bursting gems.
They made a small cry as they exploded.
"Have a nice day," Rick had said.
Soon she would feel better,
and in a few weeks
this ride could be spent reading or writing
instead of staring out the window
cataloging her failures
or reviewing the growing list
of everyone who disliked her.
A spam email arrived on her phone.
It was lineated like a poem.
She read it several times, as if
it were some urgent, sacred text
addressed only to her,

> *Recover your exceptional ID profile, benevolently check.*
> *Your yearly arrangement will before long go into outcomes.*
> *The procured request bill has been charged no further.*
> *We value your well-established authenticity in the eyes.*
> *Kindly activity tolerance while your crossing out demand is dissected.*
> *Renew your yearly help.*

It is as yet conceivable to Modernize your consumable help.
Participation was naturally broadened.
We found another rehash of credit only administrations.
Merciful immediately reauthorize your yearly arrangement, dear buyer.
Supplanting your exhausted service is fundamental.
Much obliged!
Inside a couple of seconds, your administration will initiate.
You've stirred things up around town of your proposed plan.
Be rapidly! Get your membership as quickly as could really be expected.
If it's not too much trouble, answer with us on the off chance that you
have any requests about how to drag out your entrance
or on the other hand
assuming you want direction.
and as she deleted it, she considered the ways
it exceeded her own writing,
as it was trying to move someone to do something.
Someone else's cheek, imprinted in grease
on the window made everything a blur—
shocks of clarity where the wrinkles were.
And what she'd mistook
for a dainty mound of cellophane,
a translucent slip
of plastic on the lip
of the window,
was actually a pile of acrylic fingernails
that someone who'd sat in her seat
earlier that day
had methodically removed
and placed there. It was so beautiful.
Like a mountain of tears
pushing through.

THE BEE EATER AND THE CHAMOMILE

The flowers we couldn't identify
Along the path
Turned out to be touch-me-nots
Bushes of orange and yellow holes
Exploding under the bluffs. When the cars go by
The dirt gets in them, sore-throated girls
Gossiping about the mark on his back
In the shape of Tasmania
His unwashed fingers, the way they
Shook, working over
The tortoiseshell circles
Or hooks and eyes
That open worlds

We walked along the reservoir
Was odd to think of drinking
What we saw, but
Sometimes I need to pause and
Construct images
To keep sane and remember
The surreal order of things
The water from the expensive insulated bottle
Still cold after many hours
Becoming prehistoric continents on my shirt
As I sweat through the unlined bra

You photographed the flowers
With their retreating leaves
We spoke at length about children
and dogs. And I wanted to tell you
How I thought you'd been a little mean
To J the night before
And that what you saw as her disorganization
Or scatteredness, her withdrawal, I registered
As a state of fear, fear of you, fear of failing
You. Instead, I passed you the natural repellant

Said something about how I didn't like
That I can choose any painting
From any major museum
Or historical period
And if the resolution is high enough
Can have it printed onto a pair
Of XL booty shorts
And they'll arrive at my house in 3–5 days
And if ever I am anxious
About their whereabouts, I can press
A sequence of letters and numbers
To know their every move. Across state lines
And into warehouses for holding
And redirecting. Why can't things

Just be simpler, less enmeshed?
But maybe I do like it
The tearing of the box
And what would that say

About me? My giant ass
Threatening a seam
In someone's handiwork
Or a machine's code
Blooming pigment around the crotch

A sword points nowhere. His head on a plate
Cruel heart of the painted wave, it glows
Crashes against the thigh. A scrap of red
By the horse's mouth. A servant in the corner
Of the canvas
Emerges from behind a curtain
She holds a jug of water
That she brought for you from the cellar
She isn't paying attention. It's a cool day
She is thinking of a boy, his moving throat
While last night's rain
Collects in all the low places
Of the earth

FORGETTING SOMETHING

We think, possibly, you may have left
something in your cart. Did you want
to complete your purchase?
You might regret
not possessing that
which you delicately and with care considered
from the rank enclosure of your bedroom
wrapped in a damp towel, face touched
by a taxonomic blue
from that endless river of rectangular light
by which you are carried into yourself.
A catalog enters your hypothetical flesh.
The green shape on a chain
both geometric and organic
whose purpose is only to mesmerize.
A bowl with some animal. The wash
scented with milk and crushed flowers
in which blades of heat were embedded
by the chemist's hand. He once said of you
to a mutual friend, *She's doing such impressive things*
for a woman so young. We know
you felt humors rush
toward false exits in your body.
Your desire, we suspect, is a bit like the sky
no rubber bladder, no soft border
of tissue to hold it back. "You are not yet this

but could be." Your liquid eye heaves
itself, with great difficulty, over everything
even the parallel tracks
of pebbles inlaid in the fine mud
of the road. All is customizable.
The wool cape we hold for you
is infused with the lived experiences
of a guaranteed half-dozen
promising students of art. And that resin circle
peony-shade, its yielding color
somewhat a betrayal
of its hardness, is just a click away
from taking up its new role
as window to your wrist.

SECRET SAUCE

> "The Young-Girl carries the mask of her face . . . The Young-Girl doesn't get old; she decomposes."
>
> —Tiqqun, *Raw Materials for a Theory of the Young-Girl*

FLOWER-INFUSED CLEANSING MILK
JASMINE AND LILY HEALING MASK
REDNESS RELIEF SOOTHING SERUM
SOOTHING MOISTURE MASK
CALM WATER GEL
ALL-DAY SKIN HYDRATING CREAM GEL
ANTI-POLLUTION FINISHING ESSENCE
HYDRATING PEPTIDE AND VITAMIN B5 EYE CREAM
WITH TAMARIND, SOY, WHITE MULBERRY
META CELL RENEWAL CORRECTIVE EMULSION
MINERAL EYE CREAM
HYALURONIC HYDRA PRIMER
COLORLESS FILLER
HYDRANCE AQUA-GEL
RESOLUTE HYDRATING BODY BALM
BIOLUMIN-C EYE SERUM
LUCENT FACIAL CONCENTRATE
ACTIVATED CHARCOAL MASK
PRE AND PRO-BIOTIC FACIAL MIST
ILLUMINATING ANTI-FATIGUE EYE CREAM
PINE FOREST REDEMPTION SCRUB (FOR THE BODY)

PROTINI™ POLYPEPTIDE CREAM
NIGHTLY REDEFINING MICRO-PEEL CONCENTRATE
BLACK PEPPER BETA-CAROTENE EMOLLIENT
CONCENTRATED BRIGHTENING ESSENCE
ROSEHIP BEAUTIFYING CLEANSING OIL
"ULTIMATE LIFT" M CREAM
VAGUS NERVE PILLOW MIST
WHITE STRETCH MARK EXFOLIATING AND ERASING
CREAM
DETOXIFYING NIGHT TREATMENT, ALL TYPES
TRIPLE LIPID RESTORATIVE CREAM
NORMALIZING FACE BARRIER
LIGHTWEIGHT ROSE PETAL
LAYERING SERUM
BROAD SPECTRUM MINERAL VEIL

LAVENDER LAKE

How ridiculous to start
like this, but "One day
I began to speak

almost entirely in bromides
and underneath the speaking
was a hum, a kind of liquid reverie

or mist in which questions
and ideas floated, but were
inaccessible, encased in glass

—much like the plastic eggs
from childhood, they tumbled out
of vending machines, held articulated toys,

rolls of stickers, animal images,
bits of gum or sweet dissolving
tabs—only these

were entirely sealed off
and I would hear cascading
from my mouth: *It's so good*

to see you. I'm dying
to read that. Incredibly lovely!

I'm so excited. Oh my God.

I love it. Isn't she? You look
so beautiful. Your eyes. Wow.
The way they are lined with blue.

Look at you! A sight for sore eyes.
And these pulses of language
automatic but deeply felt

and not ingenuine, were signals
from a person already dead
and I wasn't dying to do anything

because there was nowhere to go
and through the electrified air
of Brooklyn circa 2014

in which you were always being passed
or passed over, or entered, passed through
like a ghost, my lovely amazing beautiful

friends would drag my corpse to places
called Lavender Lake or Wild Birds
or Lover's Rock, One Last Shag

where I would meet men
who took me home to look at porn
or make of me a pornographic surface

the bouncing breasts projected
onto my own still ones
as I kneeled in luxury bedding

and women kissed each other
across my abdomen, and moved tenderly
the wisps of hair from each other's eyes

to reveal expressions of bewilderment
and sometimes even pleasure
and underneath was death

their built-in shelves of books
were places to look
when you couldn't look them in the eye

fair, used, rare, new, in good
condition the books held scenes of marriage,
babies, ideas, suffering, death, betrayal

in one a girl rides a little donkey
to the center of a field, the fading light
touches everything, gives flowers

and grasses and heaps of rock their icing
just before the dark gathers it all
and she's standing there still, pressed

between the light and dark. In one,
a bowl of tomatoes turns the page

into overripeness, the mother fly lands

in a gash of flesh. There's something else
half-remembered, a green scrap of talk,
or else silk, years go by inside parentheses

and I was nobody and I was beautiful
and no hammer forged would break the glass
into shards, so that I might retrieve

a morsel or shadow, and when I wanted
I could dredge them up
and show them to everyone

to the men, to my teachers, even
to you, holding their heft up to the light
to see what might be writhing inside

and now ten years have passed
and I wear mostly cotton underwear
and people ask me questions

and I teach at a university
and I read novels cover to cover
and I make my own countertop spray

by shaking the droplets from a vial
of essential oil into a larger
reusable spray bottle

containing equal parts water
and vinegar, and I am good
and I stand up in front of rooms

and words come out of my mouth
as a rash spreads across my throat
choking me from the inside

and I have published in respected magazines
I can touch my toes. I say things like
Put pressure on this stanza

or *Explore the landscape of the page*
I attend the conferences in outfits
and upload the files just in time

I called my mother tonight
to tell her that I got the test results
and I have lots of viable eggs

Isn't it amazing, she said
that all the eggs you have now
you had when you were born

They were inside you inside me
and the egg that became you
was inside me inside your grandmother

who you never met, but who everyone loved
for miles around. She fed everyone

food from her deli counter—

whatever they wanted. She cooked
steak and eggs for the farmers, the cops,
the truckers, made them feel understood

even when she was afraid, or covered
in a fine, rose-colored pain
and it goes back

and back. I wipe the counter.
It smells green—of tea tree
and eucalyptus—and I am pleased

a little, with myself, I'm not sure for what.
If I'm being honest, I just kind of fell
here, into this, through some kind of dark,

wet screen—and it's never stopped coming,
the language, the film of dust on everything,
even my books, even the words in the books

the days, the waves of tasks, the feeling
of coming so close to my own mind
but only being able to visit, as one peers into

a smudged aquarium full of dead water
in the forgotten room in someone's house
with a kind of pity for whatever animal

lives there. She's usually hiding
in her hollowed log. Sometimes it helps
if you squint through the bubbles and murk.

See the little fish darting
in and out, see the plants swaying.
Isn't she something?

A DRAPED URN

Either my eyes are slowly degenerating
(of which the doctor warned,

as early onset glaucoma
runs in the family)

or the pastel silhouettes of the dead
are using the fireplace in my room

as a kind of portal
between worlds.

My peripheral vision
chatters with movement

and forlorn shapes
trail and churn behind my gaze,

like stray cats that follow you
down the street

and would waltz right into your house
if only you'd let them.

All night small pebbles fall
down the chimney

and the floral wallpaper
seems to quake and ripple

to the beat of my breath—
the only sound around,

save for an inconstant nautical moan
that blows in from the bay. It's 4 a.m.

I am a grown adult person
gripping a flashlight

in an ancient house,
on a residency

where I'm supposed to be writing,
but am mostly online shopping,

and reading a novel,
violent and hilarious,

about an insane man and his companion,
and I think probably also

modernity
and its relationship to literature.

I've failed to adjust
to the sun's retreat

and miss the rosy noise
of the city at night,

which I experience
as a soothing rocking motion

that coaxes me
toward a sleep like death.

A shadow in the corner
looks like a demon

with a marzipan parrot
perched on his head.

I wear this feeling like a robe
that I am a ridiculous person

who will never be like the others.
(Woolf calls them "the army

of the upright," those who go
about their days

saving their money for a future
that doesn't exist, making plans

doing well at their jobs, exercising,
loving themselves and even others.)

I am one of the other ones,
the bad ones

who will never function,
scared, susceptible, lazy,

wistful. A stack of dirty dishes
and cups grows like a compressed spine

on my bedside table. And when sleep
does begin to "lower its gentle blanket

over me," as my father used to say,
I often hear a conversation

between two or three people,
as if I am being merged

into a long-distance phone call
or half-recalling a scene from Pinter.

They speak in a language
just beyond comprehension,

like if only my ears could squint
I could begin the transcription.

Last week you visited. At the cemetery,
we walked the named paths.

I saw the graves
of Longfellow, Creeley, Lowell,

and Buckminster Fuller,
a strange little dinner party.

At each grave I thought about that person
called up what I knew of them,

then let my mind wander.
We watched with love a heron

defend its statuesque
and dignified form

from a cloud of bullying blackbirds
and crouched to talk to a family

of painted turtles. I thought
about what it would be like

to have a baby together
as we looked at the outline

of a songbird, cleanly
decapitated on the grass.

The graves were many-shaped
and decorated with

sphynxes, orbs, pyramids,
garlands, animals, instruments

obelisks. One particular object
I kept noticing

as we meandered
through the symbols and names,

was a stone urn or vase
covered by a veil

that depending on the skill of the mason
was either thick and clumsy

or thin and membranous
looking like a small exhalation

could send it flying.
If I had to guess

the urn might represent the remains
of the person who has died

and the veil is the metaphysical border
that separates the living

and the dead. And if I had to diagnose
my own poems, or even myself

I might say that they (or I)
do not know what side

of anything they (or I) wish
to exist on. And maybe this is why

I am still afraid of the dark,
because I know deep down

I am jealous of the dead
and need only the slightest nudge

in order to join them
in the lushness

of their garden. The birds begin
to chirp, and the watery blue light

glows from the window
and will soon turn up

the volume on its yellows
which means the dead and I can sleep now.

I close my laptop,
abandoning my search

for the perfect Victorian nightgown
slightly sheer with a high collar

and bordered with lace,
in which I could exist

deliciously in the parlor
that separates the room

where you are a person
from that other one

where you are nothing
but a small disturbance

in the air, lint on a mantel,
voice stepping out of a jar

of day-old water.

RECEIVER

And how am I supposed

After else

A word, "green," written in red

The wet knife reaches

An arm through dark water

Her sucked idea, lonely

And which yellowed

One morning, yes

The silver utensil

As if I dreamt

The furniture showroom, full of repressed longing

Here is her review

Every page is blank!

I cannot tell you how sorry

He arrives instead, having lost all

Newt on memory of leaf, wet with stale rain

In the new architecture, nowhere to sit

I don't know what you want from me

Over the ground

The Bride of Tarantula (1967)

The legs twist, opposing in air

Pulverized stone, yes and

We found the station where statues practice their singing

As hunger follows

Unkind of me to say

Woolf says "a lump of pure sound"

Conspiring in a hive of glass

And didn't Mary call her own body

"The woman who carries me about"

I think you'd like to still me, the fumble or tremor

Sweet upon the seat

Pelvis, murky, rising to meet my face

97.5 FM, The Wound

Cream moon of her fingernail

We were at Junction Boulevard, or on it

And the trees changed their direction

Sight, my little diver

Locked drawer rattling with the complaints of gods

Forehead like a frayed calendar

And what of it

Now is under

Afraid, I—

Fisting the lilac vase for hymns

Look how I'm forgetting you, even as

All words are moved

And if I wrote what etched itself into sleep

Powdery,

Beach of her

NO PEOPLE IN IT

I flutter in order
to enter
the phrase's silver.

Jackdaws have launched nearby—
this time, silk green and ripped,
the movement a kind of chafing thinking.

Oh he's marking
terrain right there,
right there with his

unmade song. The shadow kids
whip fronds, froth air up
into heat, pure and simple

"violence of the eye." Wild lapis
ink, wet in the margin's stage.
Well, hadn't this testament begun

to carry its chime in stripes?
That's when I knew he was going away
from me, toward the sound.

Like the ring on the table
it can't be decentered.
Rim around the recent.

Ashes, ashes,
A bright tangled seeming.

EMILY

At some point in 1861, the poet began
connecting the letters in the word *the*
as one continuous line
without moving her pen from the page
and the world ended
I'm reading *The Master Letters*
from a PDF Samantha sent me
and curious about the stray marks in the left margin
of the editor's introduction, I zoom in—opening a space
between thumb and forefinger
as if releasing a gothic particle into emptiness, or examining
with a combination of adoration
and disgust, the thread
of some tacky bodily substance
stretching out between two points
—only to realize the shapes
I thought were annotations
are the fingertips of my friend, light moons
(barely there) on page 8, then absent
on 9, but on 10 I can make out
her lovely fingernails
The slight torque of her ring finger suggests
how she pressed the binding down into the glass
to ensure a clear copy, something I often do
sweating in an office
or cramped adjunct rest area

fighting a large overheating machine
that seems destined to outwit me
toward a kind of clarity and order. It's summer now
so I'm not teaching, and we never did discuss
those letters in class, as I'd assigned too much reading
a rookie habit I've never outgrown
The air is a fertile and moving liquid
I'm walking home
and the white lilies are opening
like fists inside the night
I can't look them in the center, the eye
because as you may know
you put something live in me, a hot wire
and when I admit it's there
everything will end. In the third letter
the poet's God-given heart
grows too big with love, she likens it
to a fetus outgrowing the womb
of his "little mother," or a child
growing too large to carry. On page 36
is Sam's thumb
inclining toward the word *timbrel*
It beats inside the line
written in summer
in ink, revised in pencil
in the first weeks of Civil War
I think of my friend tending
to her many alien houseplants
To be cared for like that
in the uncertainty

an end that announces itself
over and over
into our present. There's one
that looks like little chains of pills
and a rubber tree that is always fighting off death
at the edges of her leaves. One resembles a heart
or a pineapple, just squatting there
on the earth like we all do
The sky slanting in through the glass
of her cinema window. Her index
finger testing the soil
for saturation or drought
pressing down
creating its likeness
through displacement
How strong when weak
to recollect, and easy
quite, to love. The white pulp
of the screen blinks through me
Ignoring all the signs, I go
inside. I do the things I have chosen
in the lack. The amber
and green glasses in the rack
aren't quite dry, but I return them
anyway, upside down
to their very own places
to trap this meanwhile
in which you never arrive
The water pools
at every mouth
to make a little ring

TURPENTINE

We were playing WORDS.
It was a game of your devising
with no objective. We'd just had sex
rather slowly, and, I might add,
experimentally, and lay sweating
in the air conditioning, holding hands,
facing each other with eyes closed.

The sheets were inexpensive—
an abrasive violet we cratered into.

The idea, you explained, was to say a word,
but it had to be just the right one. It would come
from somewhere deep and inquisitive, must sound
meaningful inside the mouth. You cautioned me
against a kind of cleverness
to which you must have felt I was predisposed.

"Let's begin," you said, and paused
for what felt like a very long time.

"TUMBLE" you said. "CELERY"
I replied, almost instantly.

With polite tenderness, you explained
that the only rule to WORDS

was you weren't allowed to fetch your own
until after your partner had offered theirs,
as it was not a game of quick association
or one of blurting, but one of deep reflection
and slowness. I admitted

how it was difficult
for me to resist beginning to think
of my next word
immediately after I spoke one,
and you assured me this was normal,
that I could combat this tendency

by thinking of an image
or noticing a sound in the room.

But images and sounds
are attached to words, I thought.
I cannot escape them.

We moved along like this for some time,
and as you searched for your next word with a resonant calm,
I realized I could cast a red line into the dark, further and further away
from me,
and when the time came I could simply reverse the direction of the line,
which would reel in a true word, one unfettered by thinking, imagination,
or good taste.

Before this moment I'd noticed I'd tended more toward vocabulary
words, the sonically intricate, while you spoke "POOL," "TOAD," and

"HUM" into the air above my eye. It was the kind of game I wasn't exceedingly fond of, one that presented as being free of judgment but was actually impossibly judgmental. Then you said a pretty boring word I can't remember and I loved you so much.

"Do you play this when you are alone?" I asked, "This is a really weird game, and what it is keeps slipping from me." "Please, no sentences or phrases" you said. "NOONTIME."

"MOLLUSK" I said, too quickly again, regretting it almost instantly, wishing instead I'd chosen the vulgar "CLAM."

Once I'd sat at a picnic table near the place of my birth, looking out at the sea, eating a bucket of bivalves that when steamed, are commonly referred to as "steamers." Bringing one up to my face, I found a transparent worm jutting out of the grit of its belly, like a hand reaching out of a grave. Butter had dropped nauseatingly from the whole organism.

I found it was my turn again. You were taking sometimes two or three minutes to retrieve your word which I thought was a bit much, but it allowed me to go to some interesting places. I was beginning to get bored and I wanted to get up to write. I tried to clear my mind of language. To pick my next word, I went into a dark internal thicket without thinking of the word "thicket," moving shapes out of the way until I got to a clearing and something formed. It was like the moment in the movie theater where the film's title materializes slowly on the screen and you get a little chill of recognition. "That's a good one," you said. "Thanks," I said. "I'm pretty proud of it." I had waded through nothing to get here. I was at the edge of something translucent and thick. It moved a little with my breath, a living organ that went on forever. Did it shimmer? Psychoanalysts often speak of authenticity, a zone of being I've always had trouble inhabiting or conceptualizing. My high school English teacher told us never to use the word "being" in our writing. "A lazy word," she'd said. Nevertheless, I'd enjoyed its neutrality. I'd never quite been able to avoid it. You had fallen asleep.

"MOTORBIKE," I said. "GROTTO. EEL. HELLO. SILVER. TUCK. DISUSE. OSLO. SALINITY. LIMP. ORPHAN. PORNO. LOTTERY. AGAIN. SNOT. CROUCH. OVER. GLASS. AGAIN. MOTHER. PLAGUE. ASCENDING. TOWN. NOBODY. INHERIT. INGROWN. CURL. HUNTER. SNOW. THEY. DRUM. WORKER. LOG. AMBER. CUBE. FOOTSTEPS. EAR. FOUND. HERON. QUESTION. NONE." I realized then that some version of this game would likely continue for the rest of my life. I thought of the shape my mother slung over her shoulder, how I would reach inside and pull out each thing and consider it only to put it back into the hole it came from.

SO MUCH SO

The calla lily pinned to her coat
was wine-colored and open
to everything. She was falling into
a pit of spheres resembling jellied worlds.
They burst as she landed, burst
as she sank deeper, releasing objects and pictures
she could no longer name. And she was tired.
A rhythmic groaning came from underneath
it all—a sound not unlike
the one the swingset used to make
when she'd outgrown its frame.
Her legs would pierce the neon sky for hours.
Her head thrown back, the unbrushed hair
electrified and grasping. It's not that she
was going anywhere. She was just changing
her orientation to the ground and sky.
What was it called? The paper membrane
separating her from him? That country
where her family built a house
of wood and glass and increments
of speech and light? The beach she'd been to as a child
was sandless, made of millions
of smooth stones. They rattled, each
over the other, when the waves came in.
They carved their roundness in the sound they shared.
And they were sounding still, so much so,
that she could feel each one
warm and tumbling against her back.

REVERSE LULLABY

(sung by the dream mother on the other side of sleep)

If you give me just a minute
I'll rearrange the dream for you
The one you had
Where the plucked eye
Of the sun, finally sated
Rolled back its glossy form
Into the dark screen
Behind sleep

And the leopard snail
Turned her tender horns
To the underworld
Draping her leaving
Gold along the ground
For us to follow

The one where we told
Those responsible for our pain
Look, here it is, and a bright red beetle
Armored and clicking
Crawled out from the wound

And when they crushed it
Bright red powder

Stayed on their hands,
Their garments, for years

The dream in which
All we'd discarded
Came knocking, wearing garlands
Of honeysuckle, latex, and aluminum
Singing "Now what? Now what?"

And when your other mother
With her skin of glass
Reached for her sewing purse
You could see all her inside workings
Like you were peering onto the factory floor

If you give me just a minute
I'll take down your braids (she does them
So tightly) I'll pull down cameras
From the trees, rip the microphones
From the centers of flowers

I'll take the field
of sideways grasses
And place it here, where
We don't need to do anything
But wait for morning

We can stay a while
In the looping words
The letters aired out
Clean as bone

Soon the ovals will flutter open
And the nostrils suck and flare
The tin sound of a question
Rings in stale air
On the other side

Where I can't follow
The ceiling waits for you
A sheet of chalk, not without
its symbols. Dull as anything
But beautiful, certainly,
In its way

A ROOM IN DUMB BITCHVILLE

Hello. Can you hear me? If not me, do you hear the notifications sweetly intoning?
This is where I come when I'm sad or even confused. Come in. I keep adjusting the layout,

but the rooms don't seem quite right no matter what I buy. I keep the furniture quite large,
quite metallic—furry, even—and I thought to mix in a few antiques and some French tapestries

with undulating holes. There's plenty of nail polish remover and rice pudding, so help yourself.
Here, take a lusterware coupe down from the shelf. I love how heavy it feels in your hand.

I've been setting things up a little differently ever since I became what's known as a wife.
I was a girl, then I was a poet, then I was a bride. My mother fed me oysters on the porch

in my white dress of organza and open-weave linen. People kept asking me if I was cold,
but I felt lovely, like I was on ice. Like cold cream. I can't stop looking at pictures

of my happiness. His tears collected like stars in his beard. My friends, they were so beautiful.
We danced. We cut a cake. It was dry. It was the most beautiful day. The butterflies

and hawks circled against the sky. Now I'm something else, it doesn't feel quite right
in the mouth. Every room feels like a waiting room. The magazines out of date, slime blooming

in the cheap vase that holds the semiaquatic plants. My friend Simone once made a sculpture
of a woman who is in the process of becoming her own pool of tears. A lacrimarium,

it's called. Her concave abdomen was a bowl glazed with mercury. Reclining, she gazes and cries
into her hole, she becomes her hole. And what happens when she is all hole? Do you want a piece

of flourless chocolate cake? I have to be honest. I'm known for my honesty and my macramé.
All the complaints about me are true. I've let my community down. I've cried my way out

of a jam, a punishment. I've been self-sacrificing, but it's all for attention. I've been passive.
I've been dull. I've been silent and manipulative. I've taken the wrong side. At all costs,

I've avoided conflict. I've wasted time: the hours flowed like strawberry milk into the cracks
in the windows and floors. You can strike me here, if you like, on this little rectangle of flesh.

I've grown quite fond of the feeling. Like a song no one sings anymore or the pattern
on an extinct flower. Oh, you've noticed the mice, don't mind them, I can't bring myself

to cast them out, though they piss and shit little hyphens all over everything.
They are so small, and their tiny families huddle against each other for warmth.

I'm starting to think they widen the holes between things: words, days. They chew the tunnels
that connect nodes in the new thinking. Just a tug on the corner of the eye.

Their little gray forms move so fast you can barely, barely… Jesus, listen to me! I'll stop talking
about myself. Maybe I'll think instead. This is only one room in a vast conspiracy of space.

The room shows me to myself, presses on me, reflects me back. It slaps the outlines
of all it holds into focus. The borders are black and jagged. Where are my manners?

I used to curtsy, but I lost that in the collapse. I didn't lose the nod, a kind of curtsy
of the face. I still have the low bow, the unfolding of the forearm that means "after you,"

the demi-plié, the step touch, the ball change, the échappé, the heave-ho, the lunge.
I'm so lucky. Luckier than most. Whose blood is this on my turtleneck? Yours?

I can't really fix anything, but I feel all this pressure to save everyone. To be of use.
My friends, they are coming apart at the seams. Not my problem, you say?

That's where you're wrong. What if tomorrow everyone said of other people's problems
"Not my problem!" What kind of world would that be? Those clouds coming in, color of

wet newspaper, they make things feel a little episodic, like your story has been doled out
in segments on a conveyor belt, little taffy squirts of living. So we might continue

in this way, exercising our ability to slow injury, taking our great pains to glimpse
at a retreating image: the future embossed and flickering—as flies leave footprints

in the majolica. The teachers used to say, "The poem is smarter than you." Well,
I should hope so! If you must know, the toile scene is of my father, changing the batteries

in a radio at the grave of his stillborn uncle. The name on the stone is BABY. Just BABY.
I love the shit out of that dead baby. As if it were my own. And I'm the weeping willow,

repeating at the edge, though it's difficult to weep in the presence of my ancestors.
The great thing about velvet is, it shows where you've grasped it. It's a very emotional fabric.

It can *crush*. It can wear down in patterns resembling forlorn patches of earth.
You can write your pain in it. If you can do the walls in velvet, or even a dark dark suede,

you can make it so everything disappears. You don't want to disappear? I'm sorry.
I shouldn't have assumed to have pollinated your desire. Wait just here.

By the intergalactic silence of the banister. The lack of the day is violet.
I'm so glad you asked. The last thing I remember was someone, I think it was my mother,

saying: "The first thing I remember was someone, I think it was my mother."
They all groan back. A gravel sound—beauty, gray tide. I levitate in the center.

I remember the shells I would bring to her. She would thank me in her former voice,
gone now, almost light green. Wet mauve, like mouths not singing

along. Little porcelain cradles. And at one time they were everywhere.
You don't see them much anymore, do you? Lady slippers, I think they were called.

Notes

"Prelude: A Lump of Pure Sound"

A lump of pure sound

A phrase from Virginia Woolf's essay "On Being Ill." This essay is referenced throughout the book and was particularly influential in writing the final poem.

I do not have to be smart . . . I am a poet. "Poets are something else"

"Poets aren't smart. They're something else" is something I remember reading in Eileen Myles' essay "Iceland" from *The Importance of Being Iceland* (2009). The actual quote is, "In general I think writers are not smart. They are something else and each writer can fill in a word here, but smart is not what that word is." My slightly altered version of the quote has been my worry stone for over a decade and has given me great comfort.

There is a chamber of black stone. High and dry behind my stunning life.

This and "Now you've seen through me, sang the cataract" are taken from the poem "McKane's Falls" by James Merrill.

"The Duke's Forest"

Quoted text is from the poems "Dec. 28, 1974," "Song," and "Afterward," all published in James Schuyler's *The Morning of the Poem* (1980).

“An Environmental Poem”

I press against the walls / until they are curved by my curving breast / which pricks against the sharpness / of what I’ve collected / producing little pains, open words.

> This image was influenced by Gaston Bachelard’s analysis of a passage by Jules Michelet in the “Nests” chapter of *The Poetics of Space.*

“Balustrade: A Ballet in Four Acts”

This poem was commissioned by the New York City Ballet in 2020 for their *Poets of Gesture* series. It was written in dialogue with *Stravinsky Violin Concerto*, choreographed by George Balanchine.

“Tantrums in Air”

I didn’t write it. It was already there.

> A misremembered quote from Ellen Fullman’s 2009 interview for the Berkeley Art Museum and Pacific Film Archive on the development of her Long String Instrument installation and performance.

our lady has had some of her tanterums as Vapors comeing out etc.

> First recorded use of the word tantrum in 1714 in a letter from E. Verney. Thank you to Oli Hazzard for clueing me in to the word’s mysterious etymology.

“Gargouillade”

The title of this poem is the name of a very difficult, very ugly jump in ballet.

“A Potentially Good Book Soaked in Offensive Perfume”

This is a found poem, a verbatim one-star Amazon review of my first book, *Fort Not*. Punctuation has been altered for clarity.

"Voicemail from the Impaled"

This poem is in conversation with the artwork "FATEBE ROADSIDE HANG TIGHT" (2019) by Ebecho Muslimova.

"Receiver"

And didn't Mary call her own body / 'The woman who carries me about'

Something I remember reading in the Gnostic gospels.

"No People In It"

Jackdaws have launched nearby

From *Flow Chart* (1991) by John Ashbery.

"Emily"

This poem quotes *The Master Letters of Emily Dickinson*, edited by R.W. Franklin. Fingers in the margin are courtesy of poet and translator Samantha Zighelboim.

"So Much So"

This poem is dedicated to the memory of my aunt, Lynn Williams.

Acknowledgments

Poems from this manuscript have appeared or are forthcoming in the Academy of American Poets *Poem-a-Day* series, *Action Spectacle, Critical Quarterly, The Drift, Epiphany, FOLDER, Granta, Harper's, jubilat, The New York Review of Books,* the Poetry Foundation website, *The Rumpus, and The Yale Review.* Thank you to the editors of these publications.

Second books are strange animals. Thank you to Alan Felsenthal and Ben Estes for giving my work a home and making such beautiful literary objects through The Song Cave.

Special thanks to angels Daniel Poppick, Maggie Millner, and Zachary Pace, whose encouragement and brilliant eyes helped bring this book into being.

Poets and people who are a part of this book by way of conversations, guidance, friendship, mentorship, support, etc.: Samantha Zighelboim, Ali Power, Simone Kearney, Georgie Devereux, Wendy Xu, Peter Gizzi, Milla Bell-Hart, Timothy Donnelly, Dorothea Lasky, Alan Gilbert, Lynn Xu, Oli Hazzard, Ben Lerner, Chia-Lun Chang, Krystal Languell, Rachel Levitsky, Ana Paula Simões, Katie Raissian, Ry Cook, Todd Colby, Lara Mimosa Montes, Eric Dean Wilson, Jennifer Firestone,

Marcella Durand, Mia Kang, Ricardo Maldonado, Richard Deming, Nancy Kuhl, Finn Allen Anderson, and Zoë Hitzig.

Thank you to Aditi Machado, Lucy Ives, and Maggie Millner (again) for your words.

Thank you to Ebecho Muslimova for Fatebe. She has become a kind of mascot for this book. I love her.

Thank you to the Last Sundays writing group: Catherine Barnett, Patrick Gaspard, and Claudia Rankine.

I am grateful to Dana Hawkes, Clare Reihill, and Mary Rhinelander at the T.S. Eliot Foundation for running such a peaceful, inspiring, and nourishing retreat. Many of these poems emerged in conversation with the Eliot house and surrounding landscape in Gloucester, MA.

Thank you to my students, past and present, for keeping me invested in (and surprised by) what poems can do.

Hi, Mom. Hi, Dad.

Finally, thank you to my husband Alex, whose love of WORDS and ideas often stirs me into a poem. You make life weird and beautiful.

And to our little baby Blythe, about-to-be. I can't wait to meet you.

OTHER TITLES FROM THE SONG CAVE:

1. *A Dark Dreambox of Another Kind* by **Alfred Starr Hamilton**
2. *My Enemies* by **Jane Gregory**
3. *Rude Woods* by **Nate Klug**
4. *Georges Braque and Others* by **Trevor Winkfield**
5. *The Living Method* by **Sara Nicholson**
6. *Splash State* by **Todd Colby**
7. *Essay Stanzas* by **Thomas Meyer**
8. *Illustrated Games of Patience* by **Ben Estes**
9. *Dark Green* by **Emily Hunt**
10. *Honest James* by **Christian Schlegel**
11. *M* by **Hannah Brooks-Motl**
12. *What the Lyric Is* by **Sara Nicholson**
13. *The Hermit* by **Lucy Ives**
14. *The Orchid Stories* by **Kenward Elmslie**
15. *Do Not Be a Gentleman When You Say Goodnight* by **Mitch Sisskind**
16. *HAIRDO* by **Rachel B. Glaser**
17. *Motor Maids across the Continent* by **Ron Padgett**
18. *Songs for Schizoid Siblings* by **Lionel Ziprin**
19. *Professionals of Hope: The Selected Writings of* **Subcomandante Marcos**
20. *Fort Not* by **Emily Skillings**
21. *Riddles, Etc.* by **Geoffrey Hilsabeck**
22. *CHARAS: The Improbable Dome Builders* by **Syeus Mottel** (Co-published with Pioneer Works)
23. *YEAH NO* by **Jane Gregory**
24. *Nioque of the Early-Spring* by **Francis Ponge**
25. *Smudgy and Lossy* by **John Myers**

26. *The Desert* by **Brandon Shimoda**
27. *Scardanelli* by **Friederike Mayröcker**
28. *The Alley of Fireflies and Other Stories* by **Raymond Roussel**
29. *CHANGES: Notes on Choreography* by **Merce Cunningham** (Co-published with the Merce Cunningham Trust)
30. *My Mother Laughs* by **Chantal Akerman**
31. *Earth* by **Hannah Brooks-Motl**
32. *Everything and Other Poems* by **Charles North**
33. *Paper Bells* by **Phan Nhiên Hạo**
34. *Photographs: Together & Alone* by **Karlheinz Weinberger**
35. *A Better Place Is Hard to Find* by **Aaron Fagan**
36. *Rough Song* by **Blanca Varela**
37. *In the Same Light: 200 Poems for Our Century From the Migrants & Exiles of the Tang Dynasty,* translated by **Wong May**
38. *On the Mesa: An Anthology of Bolinas Writing (50th Anniversary Edition)*, edited by **Ben Estes and Joel Weishaus**
39. *Listen My Friend, This Is the Dream I Dreamed Last Night* by **Cody-Rose Clevidence**
40. *Poetries* by **Georges Schehadé**
41. *Wings in Time* by **Callie Garnett**
42. *Two Murals* by **Jesús Castillo**
43. *Punks: New & Selected Poems* by **John Keene**
44. *ABC Moonlight* by **Ben Estes**
45. *Star Lake* by **Arda Collins**
46. *The Maybe-Bird* by **Jennifer Elise Foerster**
47. *Seriously Well* by **Helge Torvund**
48. *Dereliction* by **Gabrielle Octavia Rucker**
49. *Bookworm: Conversations with* **Michael Silverblatt**
50. *April* by **Sara Nicholson**

51. *Valley of the Many-Colored Grasses* by **Ronald Johnson**

52. *The Sphinx and the Milky Way: Selections from the Notebooks of* **Charles Burchfield**

53. *Telling the Truth as It Comes Up: Selected Talks & Essays 1991–2018* by **Alice Notley**

54. *Lunar Solo: Selected Poems* by **Jules Laforgue**

55. *Stranger* by **Emily Hunt**

56. *The Selkie* by **Morgan Võ**

57. *Hereafter* by **Alan Felsenthal**

58. *Cold Dogs* by **Zan de Parry**

59. *Saturday* by **Margaret Ross**

60. *Many Poems* by **Roberta Iannamico**

61. *Ultraviolet of the Genuine* by **Hannah Brooks-Motl**

62. *Silkworm's Pansori* by **David Seung**